I0479091

THE

MINIMALIST

OF

PRACTICAL

BUSINESS

ADVICE

BE A BETTER EMPLOYEE, CO-WORKER,
COACH, MENTOR, AND BOSS

THE MINIMA**LIST** OF PRACTICAL BUSINESS ADVICE

Copyright © 2023 by Shawn Smith
All rights reserved.

to my family for their love, support... and the perspective they provide no matter what's going on in my life

to my many work colleagues for their guidance, intellect, and friendship

and a special thanks to Grace McArdle, whose kind words inspired me to write this book

AUTHOR'S NOTE

You never know where life will lead you!

I was born in the Midwest and have always called it home. I'm a husband, father of four and grandpa to two (with a third on the way). I'm an engineer by training and spent thirty-five years in industry managing projects and leading organizations. While I had, by most accounts, a successful career, I was certainly no rock star. I never sat in the corner office. I don't have an advanced degree of any kind, and I haven't consulted with industry titans. I'm just a normal guy, reasonably intelligent, curious, logical... with a heavy dose of common sense. And while I've always enjoyed passing onto others what I know, putting it into a book was never on my radar screen – until it was.

So how did this book come about? The content comes from my work experiences – the initiatives, projects, formal training, my successes, my failures, others' successes and failures, and, most importantly, the amazing people I worked with throughout my career.

The idea of documenting my advice spawned from a surprise retirement reception. One of those amazing people I reference above said some flattering things about me (as people do at such an event), recalling a few of what she referred to as "Shawn-isms" – little nuggets of wisdom I've offered as advice over the years.

The following week I was traveling and had some airport downtime. I started jotting down my learnings, opinions, observations, etc. Eventually, I compiled them into an email entitled, *"A few thoughts from a soon-to-be retired guy..."* and sent it to some of my closest work colleagues.

To my surprise, the email got forwarded more broadly and I received a number of replies thanking me for taking the time to document my thoughts. A few went a step further, stating it was the start of what could be an interesting book. It was all the encouragement I needed to take a shot at being an author.

Now, just a little over ten months into retirement, I've put the finishing touches on what I believe to be a compelling read.

My work philosophy is woven into the fabric of the book. I'm all about keeping things simple. I believe structure is important until it becomes bureaucratic. I value data and wish people would stick to the facts, not taking things so personally – it's only work. I think patience and persever-ance are undervalued in a world addicted to instant gratification. I have an appreciation for curiosity and love a good debate. I believe your business will be successful if you bring smart people with high integrity together and let them do their thing.

My confession... I can't claim to have followed each and every bit of advice, each and every day.

I did send emails at night and conducted business during my kids' soccer games. I didn't take walks routinely and did check emails right before bed. I debated too aggressively, questioned too many decisions, and didn't take the time to celebrate with others often enough.

So, I offer up this book for you to learn from my successes and a few of my shortcomings.

Shawn L Smith
April 2023

The greatest compliment you can receive is the respect of others

Respect is not something you get from holding a specific position, nor is it something you can demand. It's earned over time. It comes to those who build and promote a work environment where people are open, honest, fair, considerate of others, positive, consistent, approachable, empathetic, and inclusive.

Being respected is not the same as being popular or necessarily kind, particularly in a business setting where there are budgets, deadlines, customers, trade-offs, competing priorities, etc.

People who garner respect don't shy away from tough discussions or tough decisions. They approach them head-on and forge the best path forward.

Build your character, respect will follow.

Smart people ask for help

No matter how bright you are or how much energy and effort you've put into studying a situation, there's likely someone else who has a unique perspective or an additional piece of data that will further enhance your analysis.

Bounce your thoughts and ideas off of others. Ask for their advice and actively listen to their feedback. More often than not, you'll walk away with something you hadn't thought about or an alternative you hadn't considered.

Don't go it alone.

You have to eventually fall off the fence

I'm a huge proponent of having robust data, a solid business case, scenario analysis, discussions, debates, etc. For me, it's just good, sound business practice.

That being said, there is a day of reckoning when you have to stop analyzing and actually make a decision. You can't "straddle the fence" forever.

I've seen far too many examples of people asking for more data, more analysis, more everything – not because they actually needed it, but to put off making a decision.

Delaying a decision is a decision to delay.

It's not an apology if you try to justify it

We all make mistakes and sometimes those mistakes have a negative effect on others. An apology is a good first step in repairing damage and making amends.

However, apologies aren't easy, especially good ones. They require sincerity and an expression of regret, regardless of intent. The delivery needs to be gracious, straightforward, honest, and humble.

Saying, *"Sorry, but it wasn't my fault..."* or *"Sorry you feel that way, but ..."* is just a way for you to feel better about yourself. It does little or nothing for the person who has been hurt.

If it has a "but", it's probably not an apology.

Save time and effort – be approximately wrong, not exactly wrong

Businesses generate and rely on forward-looking data to support some of their most important business processes – e.g., business plans, strategic plans, revenue forecasts, business cases.

While it's readily acknowledged that forward-looking data is, by its nature, wrong, it doesn't stop corporations from spending an inordinate amount of time, energy, effort and resources in pursuit of excessive precision.

I've seen very smart people debate a $5 million swing up or down on a revenue projection of $300+ million five years into the future.

Don't waste your time debating numbers within the margin of error.

Don't assume "the bosses" are way smarter than you are

Far too often, I see employees, good employees, provide information to executives without a recommendation, assuming the bosses somehow know best.

On any given topic, you likely know it better than your boss (at least you should) because you've spent an abundance of time studying it, analyzing it, living it.

Be confident enough to not just assimilate and study the information, but to actually make a recommendation – accompanied by the alternatives you considered, data analyzed and the why and how you came to a conclusion.

Followers share their information with a question mark. Influencers provide recommendations.

Say thank you – often

It's such a simple thing to do. So why don't we do it more often at work?   I think it has to do with a resistance to thanking people for doing something they're being paid to do.

If we could just get over that hurdle, there are so many positives that come from a sincere "thank you". It shows people you value them and their contributions. It's motivating and encouraging and creates job satisfaction. It builds trust, promotes engagement and, ultimately, builds stronger work relationships.

The best thank yous are personal and authentic. Take the time to deliver them in person or with a handwritten note.

Don't be stingy with your thank yous. They're a great way to show your gratitude – and they're free!

Less is more... when it comes to slides

A number of years ago, a work colleague shared with me a quote attributed to Mark Twain, "I didn't have time to write a short letter so I wrote a long one instead". It stuck with me all these years and I've shared it with any number of people in the context of delivering a good presentation.

A well-drafted, crisp and concise presentation requires effort. Take the time to distill down your messages, displaying the information that matters most, while being prepared to answer questions in greater detail.

Excessive slide content draws attention away from what you're actually saying.

Curiosity is a distinguishing attribute

In my experience, the one common attribute among pretty much every "go-to" person in a given organization is curiosity.

The curious want to understand how things work, how they don't work, how things work together, how things fail, etc. They have an inherent drive, a need, a desire to learn and to connect information. As a result, they're a wealth of knowledge.

Encourage and reward people for being curious.

Jobs can be done remotely – careers are built in person

With today's technology, work can, and is, being done remotely.

That being said, remote working arrangements have their share of challenges, everything from connectivity issues to loneliness to a general lack of interaction. And it's certainly more difficult to feel connected to a corporate culture when you're confined to a home office.

Careers are heavily influenced by networking, relationships, familiarity, visibility, and mentoring – things experienced more readily with physical presence.

Routinely connect with influential people, in person.

Can you really multitask?

In short, "no". Humans just aren't wired to focus on more than one thing at a time. When you think you're multitasking, you're actually switching your attention from one task to another extremely quickly. You're not giving anything your full attention.

Multitasking decreases your efficiency as well as performance. In an attempt to get more things done, you're actually getting less done, while the quality of your work suffers.

Face it, you can't actively participate in a meeting while reading emails. You can't follow a recipe and talk to your best friend on the phone. And you certainly can't drive and text, or even walk and text.

Tackle one task at a time, well.

Challenge bad news –
really challenge good news

Good news is welcomed. Bad news... not so much.

The bearer of bad news knows their message is not what people want to hear. They know preparation is key for the inevitable challenge they'll receive. As a result, they immerse themselves in the details and know the data, ensuring their analysis is on solid footing.

Conversely, the deliverer of good news knows it's unlikely they'll be challenged. They know they can pass off aspirations as data in support of a largely superficial analysis. People inherently want to believe their story. What good would come from challenging it?

Over time, people realize good news is an easy path to accolades, especially when the benefits are projected out well into the future, well beyond any personal burden of accountability.

Make people soundly justify their good news.

The only question you'll definitely not get answered is the one you don't ask

To really get to know a topic – a company, a product, your employees' career aspirations, etc. – you need to probe, you need to investigate.

Don't be afraid to ask questions. The worst thing that can happen is the person refuses to answer – and sometimes that's an answer in itself.

Don't provoke a quick "no" – plant a seed

When it comes to influencing decisions, you need to be keenly aware of your working environment. How much support or opposition is there for your position? Where is the key decision maker leaning? When does the decision need to be made?

There are certainly times when it's appropriate to drive hard for a quick decision – e.g., you sense there's broad support for it.

There are other times when it pays to be patient, introducing an idea or initiative without immediately driving for a decision – i.e., planting a seed. It gives people a chance to catch up and learn more about the initiative and affords you the opportunity to lobby for it off-line.

Be patient. Some decisions just aren't meant to be made today.

Make sure your boss knows what you do and what you've accomplished

Routine one-on-ones with your boss afford you the op-portunity to interact, regardless of how things are going.

In preparation, jot down an informal agenda to ensure you cover the most important things. Use the bulk of your time to:

- Provide project updates
- Review business performance and metrics
- Highlight accomplishments
- Gain alignment
- Ask for input/feedback
- Discuss career opportunities

Quality "boss time" is limited – use it wisely.

Never ever check your phone while meeting with someone

… unless you've given them a heads-up you're expecting an important call or text.

Admitting you don't know something makes you more human, more authentic

We've all experienced that "special person" who has an answer or solution for anything and everything, even when it's painfully obvious they don't.

Don't be that person – readily admit you don't have the answer when, in reality, you don't. In other words, be honest.

People don't expect you to know everything.

It's more than okay to say "not now" to good ideas

Prioritization is probably the single most challenging thing for organizations to get right. There are a lot of great ideas and a lot of sponsors wanting their projects at or near the top of to-do lists.

Unfortunately, there is a finite resource pool available to support new initiatives. And there's only so much change an organization can absorb at any given time.

New initiatives should only be undertaken as others are completed, and the pace and sequence of change needs to be carefully monitored and managed.

Working on all things at the same time is a good way to get none of them completed.

When negotiating, an awkward pause or silence isn't a bad thing

A formal negotiation is a stressful activity for most everyone, as it's inherently confrontational. Don't let stress manifest itself into nervous habits, including the need to fill gaps in the conversation.

If you've posed a question or pointed out an inconsistency in a person's position and they're not answering, let the silence linger. The ball is in their court.

Don't negotiate against yourself by breaking the silence.

A revenue projection is not a business case

If I had a dollar for every time someone said they had a "positive business case" because they could generate $x millions of peak sales by implementing an initiative... I'd have a bunch of dollars.

Understanding potential revenue is a good place to *start* a business case, but it also needs to factor in the upfront development costs, the cost to make the product, the cost of generating sales, etc.

Proposed initiatives need to bear the full brunt of their projected implementation and operating costs.

Just because your spreadsheet can handle numbers with lots of decimal points doesn't mean you should show them

Spreadsheets are powerful tools capable of handling thousands or millions of calculations, but they can't improve the accuracy of your underlying data.

When your spreadsheet displays a revenue projection five years into the future of $23,073,232, it doesn't mean you're capable of predicting sales to the nearest dollar. If you have a rough estimate of capital, it can't be $72.253 million. It's approximately $70 million.

Don't display data in a way that insinuates far more precision than is actually known.

Every company should have a Commonsense Committee

... or at least adopt a commonsense mindset.

Contrary to what you've likely been told, there are such things as "bad ideas" and, yes, there are times when these "bad ideas" get traction and are brought forward for support and funding.

If a Commonsense Committee were, hypothetically, to exist, these "bad ideas" would be wholly rejected as monumental wastes of time and resources.

When things come forward for approval, think about how they'd play in the Commonsense Committee.

NOTE: The one qualification for being a member of the Commonsense Committee (if one were to exist) is the person nominated would NEVER want to be on ANY corporate committee.

Sleep is a prerequisite to productive waking hours

Peak performance of anything, including work, requires both your body and your mind to be rested. The average person needs 7-8 hours of quality sleep for healing, regulating, and restoring the body.

The lack of consistent sleep can lead to brain fog, low energy, moodiness and ultimately an increased risk of health issues.

Never check your email or texts right before bed. Do you honestly believe previewing tomorrow's work challenges is an effective sleep aid?

Establish a good sleep routine and stick with it.

Don't let arrogance be your downfall

Come on, just admit it.

- You're not the smartest person in every room
- The world doesn't actually revolve around you
- You don't win every time
- You're not better than everyone else
- You're wrong some of the time
- There's at least one thing you're sorry for
- It's very unlikely you're the most (or least) of anything, as there are over eight billion people on this planet

It's good to be confident and have high self-esteem, just don't overdo it.

Upgrade your arrogance to grace and humility.

Your best attribute in excess is likely your greatest weakness

Everyone has their strengths and weaknesses. You're at your best when work activity is in line with a particular strength. But when that strength is excessive, it can be problematic.

Javier excels at driving activity *(good thing)*, until he drives everyone crazy *(not so good)*.

Bob loves to debate *(strength)*. Bob loves to win a debate at all costs *(weakness)*.

Susie values data and statistical analysis *(good thing)*, but struggles making decisions *(bad thing)*.

Be conscious of how your best attributes on steroids manifest themselves.

The greatest compliment a technical expert can receive shouldn't be a management position

Technical experts add tremendous value to an organization. They invent things, deliver capital projects, drive process optimization, etc.

Leadership doesn't come exclusively from managing people. Leading a project or process often yields comparable or greater value to managing people.

Nurture and reward your technical experts.

You can't say you're on _____ if you don't have one

You can't say you're on <u>plan</u> if you don't have one.

You can't say you're on <u>schedule</u> ...

You can't say you're on <u>budget</u> ...

Planning is a guide to action.

The work that goes into developing and networking a plan leads to a better overall understanding of the current state and is the basis for future optimization.

The lack of planning can lead to confusion, shortages, delays, cost overruns, low productivity and ultimately low employee morale.

Establish and document goals and routinely monitor progress to drive accountability.

Strive for consistency

Be predictable in your behaviors and work output, building trust and establishing a positive reputation.

- Treat your employees and co-workers *consistently* – creating a healthy work environment built on a foundation of fairness and accountability

- Supply *consistently* high quality products and services to customers – providing an excellent customer experience and building brand loyalty

- *Consistently* meet deadlines and goals – delivering value, while enhancing your credibility

- Take a *consistent* approach to analyzing and evaluating data – reducing the risk of making biased or uninformed decisions

- Execute work processes *consistently* – establishing a baseline of performance

Consistency allows for measurability... which is the first step toward improvement.

You're unlikely to get to your career destination without a map

Do you have career goals? If so, what are they? What do you envision yourself doing 10-15 years in the future? Do you see yourself in upper management? Are your interests aligned with being a technical expert? Are you content in your current field or industry?

Assess your strengths and foundational experiences relative to your goals. Determine what work experience and/or skill gaps you need to address to be a viable, competitive candidate for your "destination role".

Document a boss-aligned career map.

Schedule uninterrupted time – it doesn't happen naturally

When dealing with a particularly challenging assignment, you need to carve out time to think things through, consider options, analyze data, etc. To do it well, you need a stretch of time free of distractions.

Unfortunately, real life imposes barriers. Full calendars take up your time. The open office layout is distracting. And technology – email, instant messaging, texts, etc.– is disruptive.

Put "think time" on your calendar, find a location with limited traffic or a door, and silence your electronics.

There's nothing wrong with a judgment call – just don't make people invent data to support it

Business leaders are tasked with making tough decisions. And some of these decisions are more visionary, not conducive to the analysis and measures used to justify a "normal opportunity". The opportunity may be highly risky, or the outcome binary – it's a clear winner or a total bust.

In these cases, it's okay to make a judgment call. I assume many of the most successful business ventures were judgment calls.

Trust your instincts.

Do you demonstrate a work/life balance?

While this isn't a new issue, it's never been so hard to unplug from the office and strike a good balance between your work and family life.

Studies show people are more productive when they prioritize a healthy personal life. What do your work practices say about your priorities?

What time do you arrive at work? Leave work? Do you send emails and texts during evening hours? Do you take vacations – real vacations? Do you work on weekends? Do you take calls during your daughter's soccer game?

Routinely disconnect to (1) re-energize and (2) give those around you permission to do the same.

Save meeting time by recognizing when you're in violent agreement

In science, there's a well understood principle that gas expands to fill the space in which it exists. There must be a similar corollary referencing meeting topics filling the allotted time.

How often have you been engaged in a discussion, one that's lasted far too long, only to realize the individuals or the entire group are actually pretty well aligned – but somehow finding ways to prolong the discussion?

Don't be afraid to end a meeting early.

If someone has to tell you they're being ___, it's because they're typically not

Fill in the blank with transparent, humble, vulnerable, empathetic, honest, generous, or any number of other positive attributes.

I'm a firm believer your actions define who you are. They demonstrate what you value and how you think people should be treated. No amount of talk is going to convince people you're actually different than your latest action.

Consistently demonstrate the traits you want to be known for.

The message is more important than the slides, but you do want to look professional

Don't lose sleep over your font selection or whether you use round or square bullet points. And certainly, don't waste time automating slide transitions and moving objects.

That being said, you do want your presentation materials to represent and enhance your message.

Make sure the slides are organized, clear/concise, readable and are free of typos and other errors. Graphical representation of data can be a nice upgrade to a complicated data table, especially if trends are important.

Don't let sloppy slides overshadow your otherwise brilliant message.

Encourage and reward replication

Oftentimes, people feel they're doing their best work when they devise new and different ways of doing something. It allows them to show off their skills, their abilities, their creativity, etc.

However, in practice, the best solutions may actually be those that are already being employed elsewhere within your company or industry. While they may not be sexy, they work and have stood the test of time.

Steal shamelessly, putting your energy into flawless implementation.

Be a bit skeptical of percentages

I see this so often in the news media, "There's been a 40% rise..." in this or that over some period of time.

A percent increase or decrease is only meaningful in the context of a starting point.

For example, if an old man's entire net worth was a dollar and he subsequently found a five-dollar bill on the ground, the headline would read, "A man in New York increased his net worth by 500% while walking down 42nd Street".

People "abuse" percentages to sensationalize their message when the true, absolute value is less than compelling.

Ambiguity in the workplace is inevitable – you better get comfortable navigating it

Ambiguity exists anywhere there's a lack of clarity. In the workplace, it's an assignment with a vague goal, a new organizational structure with yet-to-be-defined account-ability, or an initiative supported by incomplete information.

The difference between success and failure lies in your ability to effectively deal with this uncertainty. It's about learning to act without knowing all the details and confi-dently taking risks. It's about trying something new without knowing it will be successful.

In the face of ambiguity, assess the available data, ask plenty of questions and then take your best stab at setting a direction. Monitor the situation as more is known and adjust course, as needed.

Stagnation is the product of needing perfect information or crystal-clear direction.

Don't give your boss permission to do your job

You've probably experienced it at one time or another – a boss getting overly involved in your work. They may have the best of intentions or may not even realize they're doing it, but they are... they're doing YOUR job, unsolicited.

Be upfront with your boss, "I'm letting you know something is going on, but don't need your direct involvement".

Communicate decisions as soon as possible

A couple things happen once a decision is made.

1. The answer, "We're still looking into it", is no longer an option.

2. It's hard to maintain confidentiality, as people like to talk.

In the absence of transparency and clarity, people fill in the blanks with scenarios which are oftentimes worse than what is actually happening.

Get ahead of rumors to maintain employees' trust.

Enjoy a good debate, then go to lunch

I'm a firm believer that good debates lead to the best decisions.

For a debate to be effective, both sides need to be passionately represented. A simple pros and cons coming from a single source is not a debate.

People who enjoy a good debate (and are good at it), don't take it personally. They "go to lunch" with the very person they just tried to eviscerate. They view debate as an opportunity to take a stand, while actively listening to others' perspectives and learning from the exchange of ideas and positions.

Find ways to incorporate active debate into your decision-making processes.

Integrity is non-negotiable

Integrity involves doing the "right thing" even when no one's watching. It's personal to you and is heavily influenced by your value system and beliefs. It's the basis of your reputation and the core of your brand.

People of high integrity draw others to them, as they are reliable, trustworthy, and take commitments seriously. They can be counted on to behave in a way that represents your company in a positive light.

Don't compromise your principles for short-term gains.

Cherish feedback, especially the constructive variety

While constructive feedback can be hard to hear, it's vitally important for your development. It gives you insights into those areas holding you back and provides specific actions you can take to be more effective.

Don't take feedback too personally. Take it as a compliment you have the kind of relationship that can withstand such an interaction.

Always thank the person giving you feedback – they're the ones that actually care.

What gets tracked, gets done

To ensure things get done, you really need to have some sort of a "to-do" list – for yourself and for any group or team you facilitate. A simple reminder of assignments can do wonders when it comes to driving accountability.

Your to-do list doesn't have to be sophisticated. It simply needs to

1. Be visible

2. Track the task, due date, task owner, and status of the action

3. Be routinely reviewed, noting those tasks that have been completed and/or reprioritized

Find satisfaction in getting things done and marking them off your to-do list.

You spend time on the things you care about most

Your time is a valuable commodity. In fact, it's probably your most valuable commodity. It's finite. You can't buy more and, once lost, it can never be replenished.

Use your time wisely. From a work perspective, focus your time and energy on those things that most contribute to your company's goals, and find ways to minimize or ignore unnecessary tasks or projects.

Bosses, your most important goals should be associated with developing people, ensuring your organization is capable and putting robust succession plans in place.

If someone actively tracked your time, what would it say about you?

Don't recognize your team with a key ring – or a crystal paper weight

No one feels particularly appreciated when they receive a recognition trinket.

If you want to truly recognize an individual or group for their accomplishments, you need to make it more substantial (big money is always appreciated) or more personal. More personal typically draws on more of your time – time that doesn't go unnoticed by those being recognized.

Invest in meaningful recognition. A half-hearted attempt will be seen as just that.

Action is the precursor to motivation

All achievements start with an action.... which is, in turn, motivating, causing further action and ultimately results.

Don't just talk about what you want or need to do, actually do it. Take a first step, even if it's a small one.

Waiting to get motivated is exactly that... waiting.

Treat people the way you want to be treated

The Golden Rule... so simple, yet so powerful.

If we could all just follow it!

Channel your inner calm

There are any number of positives that come from individuals, particularly leaders, staying calm, even in the direst of situations.

Calmness exudes a sense of confidence and reassurance that everything is going to be okay. It helps people stay focused instead of jumping to worst-case scenarios. It facilitates crisp and clear communications and helps people respond rather than react. It promotes rational thought.

Put "calm" in your arsenal when dealing with particularly stressful matters.

Of course office politics exists

Politics of one sort or another exists in virtually all organizations – kids' sports, school boards, churches, government, judicial systems, etc. Why wouldn't it exist in your work setting?

Political intelligence helps you understand how relationships are related to decision making. It affords you the opportunity to interact with people who have the power to advocate for your ideas and for your career.

Being political doesn't mean you're selling out or your actions have to be at the expense of others. It's about building relationships and exercising influence.

Set your sights on being politically savvy.

You can't save your way to prosperity

Cutting costs and harvesting synergies are good ways to drive short to mid-term, improved performance.

That being said, they have their limits, both in how much they can actually deliver and in how much an organization can handle and stay engaged.

Cost cutting is the tweaking around the edges – it's hardly a substitute for innovation.

Don't blindly trust the data

People can easily manipulate and display data to support whatever point or conclusion they're wanting to promote.

If you want to claim diets cause weight gain, just look at the average weight of people on diets and compare it to those that aren't.

You need to understand the context of your data, where it came from and how it's displayed. A simple change of scale on a chart can make a meaningless blip in the data look like a game-changer.

Know your data's pedigree before using it.

The 80/20 Rule is alive and well

The 80/20 Rule, aka the Pareto Principle, was developed by Italian economist Vilfredo Pareto in the late 1800's. He grew peas in his garden and noticed that 80% of his harvest came from just 20% of the pea pods.

Applied more broadly, The 80/20 Rule states that 80% of the results arise from just 20% of the inputs.

- 80% of a company's sales are derived from just 20% of their customers
- 80% of healthcare costs are administered to 20% of the patients

Taking an "80/20 Mindset" can help when it comes to allocating limited resources.

Apply the bulk of your effort to a small number of your best initiatives, customers, products, etc.

A valiant effort isn't a good excuse for missing the target

There's no place for participation trophies in business. Just because you labored hard over a project doesn't mean you advanced it.

This is not to say there's a total lack of appreciation for putting forth effort, as there can be learning from falling short of the goal... but it's still falling short of the goal!

You wouldn't give accolades to your cardiothoracic surgeon for "trying hard" on your triple bypass. And you wouldn't give positive reviews to a chef for all his efforts "trying" to get your steak cooked just right. Why should your job be any different?

Don't expect to be rewarded for how hard you try.

Think about how the message will land – before you deliver it

Consider your audience. How might they react to the news you're preparing to share? Is it likely to be viewed positively? Negatively? Will the group be surprised? Will they be confused? Will some view it as unfair? Will there be cheering? Dissatisfaction? Indifference?

Anticipate reactions and questions to aid in your message preparation.

Give books sparingly, with intent

I can't tell you how many times throughout my career, I, along with many of my work colleagues, were gifted the latest-and-greatest business or leadership book. The gift often came with little context and no specific expectation of doing anything with it. And as you might expect, many of those books ended up on a cubicle shelf, unread, gathering dust.

There's obviously some very insightful content in any number of books and publications currently available. And any one of them may be exactly what your business needs. That being said, it can be distracting to an organization to chase the latest business trend or management tool.

Be selective of the business content you promote – much of it will end up being yesterday's fad.

NOTE: This book is a notable exception to the above. It's absolutely okay to broadly distribute it... in fact I encourage it!

You're smart – but are you emotionally intelligent?

Emotional intelligence is the ability to perceive, evaluate, express and control emotions.

People with high emotional intelligence:

- Think about feelings
- Have high self-awareness
- Accept and embrace change
- Manage emotions in difficult situations
- Demonstrate empathy
- Are self-motivated
- Express genuine and authentic concern
- Understand they benefit from criticism
- Take responsibility for their actions
- Readily let go of mistakes
- Think before reacting

Be aware of the emotional impact your actions have on others – and yourself.

Hope is not a strategy

... and neither is forcing people to change future projections to get to an answer or output that is more palatable.

If the numbers don't add up, you can't "hope" them away – you need to intentionally change something.

Laziness is a half-baked idea disguised as creativity

Just to be clear, I have no issues with the brainstorming of creative ideas or solutions as the *starting point* for a great initiative or project.

The problem arises when a half-baked idea gets traction as an implementable project with little challenge or definition. This, in turn, causes others to either (1) do the real work to scope and implement the project or (2) spend time and effort convincing the decision maker it really isn't a great idea, no matter how it was originally pitched.

Make sure initiatives are well defined before approving them for implementation.

Don't approach financial negotiations with a win/win mindset

I know this goes against deal-making conventional wisdom – to always look for win/win solutions.

In general, I agree partnerships should be built on a foundation where both parties "win". However, when it comes to specific financial terms, a dollar in your pocket is a dollar out of the other party's pocket.

Be a stingy negotiator. The other party will always be more than happy to take your money if you let them.

Activity does not equal progress

It's shocking how much non-value-added activity is generated when businesses are confronted with adversity. Instead of thinking things through, employees feel compelled to act now, to call meetings, to implement half-baked ideas, etc.

Just because people or organizations are busy, doesn't mean they're making progress.

Misguided activity is wasted activity.

When probing for information, ask broad, open-ended questions first

People tend to start their due diligence of an opportunity by asking very specific questions, to which they get very specific answers. These questions, while detailed, have little depth and are self-limiting to the questioner's knowledge and experiences.

Asking open-ended questions puts the burden of scoping the answer on the person actually answering it. It's amazing the amount of information people divulge when they're left to their own devices.

People like to talk about what they know — put them in the perfect position to do it.

It shouldn't be easy to make money – and usually isn't

People are always looking for easy money, an easy answer, a silver bullet, etc. – and corporations are no different.

How many times have you been asked to come up with just one or two things that could materially change the trajectory of your company? If it were that easy and that obvious, we should all be fired for not finding it before the question was posed.

Do the hard work to drive incremental, continuous, improvement across numerous opportunities.

Don't surround yourself with only like-minded people

It's human nature – people like to be around others with similar backgrounds, similar interests, and similar thought processes. It makes for a comfortable work environment with minimal conflict and easy decisions.

But like-mindedness breeds groupthink, where maintaining loyalty becomes more important than making the best choices and consensus wins out over critical thinking.

Diversify your inner circle.

Be assertive, not aggressive

Assertiveness is an admirable trait. It manifests itself as clear and direct communication of a person's views and positions. The messaging is confident, polite, and calm, delivered in a constructive manner, considering and respecting the views, feelings and beliefs of others. It's never rude or offensive.

Aggression, on the other hand, is angry, attacking and threatening. It has a know-it-all attitude that is dominating and commanding. It gives little consideration to others' needs. "It's my way or the highway" is its motto.

Assertiveness sits in the perfect position between passivity and aggression. Use it to clearly state your views.

You can't "entitle" your way to success

Success is earned, as is respect, a promotion, a raise, and even the opportunity to work for a company.

Entitled individuals believe they should get something because of who they are, not because of what they've accomplished. They believe privileges and perks are rights and expectations. They expect accolades for their work no matter what the outcome and view constructive feedback as a personal attack.

Entitlement is self-serving. It degrades collaboration and breeds organizational mediocrity.

Expect only what you've earned.

Work may be the most stable part of an employee's life

We all have a work life and a home life – hopefully you're able to largely segregate the two.

Unfortunately, when someone is dealing with a particularly stressful situation at home (e.g., sick child, unexpected expenses, failing relationship), it bleeds across the work-life boundary. In these cases, work may very well be a person's safe haven.

Be conscious of how even small changes to your work environment may affect those in a fragile state.

Know your numbers

Business is all about the numbers – sales dollars, sales volume, yields, expenses, product potency, inventory value, cost of goods, return on investments, etc.

How well do you understand the data you're responsible for? Is it trending in the right direction? Do you know how it relates to the profitability of the company? Is it aligned with your Business Plan?

Dive into the details and keep score.

When contemplating a new initiative, consider how easy or hard it will be to maintain

Most projects are approved with a reasonable scope and a goal to make the solution as simple as possible. However, as projects progress through design and implementation, oftentimes scope creeps and designs get overly complex.

With system complexity comes the need for extensive, ongoing support, long after project teams have disbanded.

As projects are reviewed, continually assess whether the level of support needed to maintain a system is justifiable.

Make "readily sustainable" a project design criterion.

Be attentive

When a co-worker has taken time out of their busy schedule to meet with you, it's important you're not only physically present, but you're giving the conversation your full, undivided attention – blocking out distractions, making eye contact, actively listening, etc.

Your attentiveness shows the other person they matter and what they're telling you matters. It conveys a sense of recognition.

If you can't be attentive, reschedule.

Aspirations have their place – just don't make them your plan or business case

An aspiration is a strong desire, one that lacks a defined pathway to be achieved. There's no explanation of how to get to it or when, just that it's important to attain – someday.

Conversely, a plan is grounded in reality with a relatively high degree of certainty it can be achieved within a defined timeline. It's measurable and specific and an organization can readily commit to it.

Don't promise something you're unlikely to deliver.

Don't let corporate-speak be your second language

We've all used it, accidentally or on purpose. Regardless, it's time to do away with that annoying business jargon that permeates the workplace.

- We certainly don't need a paradigm shift to put lipstick on a pig.

- Giving 110% won't prevent us from eating the elephant or boiling the ocean.

- We can't ideate ourselves to the next level by thinking outside the box, even if we believe it's mission critical.

- If we hit the ground running with all hands-on deck, we just might be able to harvest some low hanging fruit or trim some fat in an effort to move the needle, but it won't be a game changer.

Pivot to a new normal... just say what you mean or what you want in the simplest terms possible.

Ask for challenging assignments

There's no better way to show people you're capable of a higher-level position than to consistently deliver on challenging assignments in your current role.

Challenging assignments stretch your abilities, add to your knowledge base, expand your network and demonstrate versatility and flexibility. They show you can readily handle the pressure that accompanies high profile, weighty assignments.

A challenging assignment is one of the highest forms of recognition an employee can receive – ensure your boss knows it.

Make challenging assignments your Development Plan.

Influence enables you to deliver value well beyond your pay grade

Formal authority and influence come from holding a particular position. Informal influence comes from who you are and how well you motivate people to support your initiatives and adopt your ideas.

You build influence by:

1. Focusing on what you do control and consistently delivering results, building trust and a positive reputation

2. Being assertive, ensuring your ideas get visibility

3. Capitalizing on strong relationships

Success at the office is largely dependent on people *wanting* to follow you.

Promote and reward *educated* risk taking

Taking risks is not a lazy, sloppy or cavalier endeavor. On the contrary, a lot of work goes into understanding a situation well enough to take a risk – an *educated* risk.

Managing risk is about knowing what you don't know. It's about trying everything possible to eliminate or minimize potential failures. And it's about assessing the potential payoff relative to the possible loss.

Only take risk when an associated, understood, proportional benefit is probable.

Build a strong network

Routinely connect with people, internal to your company and more broadly. Really get to know them, providing assistance where you can and potentially getting help in return.

Take advantage of the many benefits derived from effective networking.

- Strengthen business connections
- Share fresh perspectives and ideas
- Exchange career advice and support
- Gain knowledge
- Explore job opportunities

Take an authentic interest in other people.

Negotiate a contract like it's a divorce settlement

A lot of people approach contract negotiations with a mindset that the deal will be wildly successful for both parties – forever! As a result, a bulk of the negotiation and associated contract language centers on how to manage success.

Unfortunately, that's not how contacts get used in the real world. When things are going well, contracts largely sit on shelves, collecting dust.

Contracts are retrieved and reviewed when things go south, when the parties cease to see value and are generally not getting along. Lawyers from both sides sift through contract language looking for provisions that give their company rights to whatever value remains (obviously at the expense of the other party).

Protect your long-term interests by negotiating contract language covering a failing partnership.

Assign someone to "connect the dots"

A vast majority of problems, initiatives, projects, etc. require cooperation across multiple functions, geographies, and potentially companies.

As an example, when a company contemplates the introduction of a new product, Research needs to invent and develop it. Manufacturing needs to figure out how to make it. And Sales and Marketing needs to identify who to sell it to and for how much.

If these functions do their work in isolation, there will almost certainly be disconnects, inconsistencies, and conflicts.

Don't assume functions will naturally cooperate with one another.

Does it practically matter?

Individuals, teams, and, more broadly, businesses, waste a lot of energy and effort contemplating and sometimes acting on scenarios that don't exist and have never happened – but *might* just happen going forward, i.e., hypothetical situations.

Be sensitive to discussions and debates that go down a "what if" path too far. Bring the group back to reality. Is it a scenario that is at least somewhat likely to happen?

Spend time on those things you can reasonably act on.

Relationships still matter – maybe now more than ever

While we're all getting more comfortable using electronic communications, we're still human. And humans are social beings, needing connections with others – needing relationships.

Good working relationships improve collaboration and employee morale, build trust and a sense of community, and enhance the on-boarding of new employees. Loyalty is built through relationships and is a main reason why employees stay at a company.

Take the time to routinely connect with your co-workers.

Don't underestimate the damage a bad employee can do

A single employee with a poor attitude and bad work ethic can poison an entire organization. The cost of retaining such an employee extends well beyond their direct compensation. Collateral damage can be extensive.

- Lower overall morale as the rest of the team has to pick up the slack

- Motivation drain – a perception there are few or no consequences for poor performance

- Increased friction, tension, hostility, drama

- Loss of confidence in leadership

- Management distraction, as they deal with discipline and training issues

Don't let poor performers loiter.

Make reliability your *wow factor*

Whaaat!? Reliability a *wow factor*? Shouldn't it be a basic expectation when someone commits to do something? Of course, the answer is "yes", but, unfortunately, in today's world reliability seems to have become the exception.

People are constantly overpromising and underdelivering. They gain business or opportunity with hype, only to disappoint in execution. They have to be reminded of their commitments and supervised in their delivery.

Differentiate yourself... commit to a job well done and reliably deliver on that commitment.

Routinely take walks throughout your workday

Don't strap yourself to a desk or get holed up in a conference room. Find excuses to get up, get out and stretch – both your physical and mental health will benefit.

Be creative.

- Park well away from your office
- Use the stairs instead of an elevator
- Walk to the cafeteria or a nearby restaurant for breaks and lunch
- Take a call while taking a stroll
- Use the bathroom on another floor or the building next door

Take the steps necessary to get your necessary steps.

Trust but verify

I was first introduced to this concept when I started taking part in the due diligence of business development opportunities – e.g., acquisitions, in-licensing deals.

At the kick-off meeting, the diligence leader emphasized the importance of really getting to know a company, their products, their technologies, etc. He said the target company needed to do more than just *talk* about how great they are, they also needed to provide *tangible evidence* in order for an investable conclusion to be drawn.

Trusting but verifying doesn't just apply to business development opportunities or external companies. Internal decisions need robust data and, as such, can benefit from the verification of information.

Unsubstantiated information is little more than a rumor.

Good business decisions aren't necessarily good for each and every employee

Businesses are constantly faced with decisions, in many cases tough decisions – e.g., how to proceed with a product launch, where to add manufacturing capacity, how much inventory to hold.

Some of these decisions are broadly positive, good for company performance and good for the employee base. But more often than not, decisions come with trade-offs. Adding capacity at one manufacturing site negates the need for another site. Deploying sales reps for a new product launch requires downsizing of an existing sales force.

Be empathetic, but don't let your emotions get in the way of the right decision.

Don't put off dealing with your procrastination problem

For starters, you need to acknowledge that any given task is (1) not going to resolve itself and (2) not going to be any easier to complete at a later date.

Procrastination is typically not a time management issue, but more about avoiding an unpleasant task, a general lack of interest, a feeling there's little value in completing the task, or a fear of failure.

While tasks age on your to-do list (assuming you have one), your anxiety increases.

Get started on those festering tasks. You might be surprised how easy they are to resolve.

Unfortunately, you have to allocate resources to maintain current performance

It's easy to get excited about constructing a new facility, launching a new product, implementing a new IT system, or acquiring a new customer. But you can't forget about all the facilities you already own, the products you already sell, the IT systems you've already deployed or the customers you already serve.

Your existing business needs continued attention (i.e., investment) to maintain status quo performance. Neglect will almost certainly lead to decay.

Budget for the maintenance of your existing assets.

When in doubt, over-communicate

I can't think of a single instance throughout my career when people complained about getting too much information or being subjected to too many communications.

People, in general, like knowing what's going on, how the company is performing, key issues facing the business, competitive pressures, priorities, challenges, etc. It's far better to communicate what is known in a timely manner, even if it's incomplete.

Exploit multiple forms of communication, mixing things up – e.g., town halls, emails, one-on-ones, small group meetings, newsletters.

Communicate often, personalize your message and leave time for questions.

There's no way to rebut constructive feedback without coming across defensive

It's just not possible. You're not going to debate your way out of whatever feedback or advice the person has taken the time, effort and risk to deliver to you.

So, what to do?

1. Shut up and listen
2. Play back what you've heard
3. Ask clarifying questions
4. Thank them for being open and honest
5. Follow up at a later date to discuss how you're addressing their feedback

Taking feedback defensively is a good way to never get it again.

Meetings aren't free

There's a very real cost to convene a meeting and an implicit expectation of extracting value from it. Value comes in the form of plans and/or decisions derived from the group having discussed differing perspectives on a given topic.

Attending meetings isn't a spectator sport. If you've been extended an invitation, there's a presumption of presence, preparation and active participation.

Before scheduling a meeting, ask yourself a few questions:

- Is the meeting absolutely necessary, or is there a more efficient way to get to the same outcome?
- Are each of the attendees required, or just nice to have?
- How much time is really needed?

Be purposeful when scheduling peoples' time.

Don't provoke unnecessary discussion by providing unnecessary information

Some people feel compelled to share any and all infor-mation, data, and analysis they've explored. In other words, they share too much.

Transparency is a good thing. But in a work setting where there is limited time to discuss issues and make decisions, it can be a distraction, sending the conversa-tion in multiple directions and diverting attention away from the salient points.

Provide information specific to your proposal and keep the rest to yourself, as back-up.

Visualize potential outcomes as part of your decision-making process

When contemplating a decision, map out the range of possible outcomes. Start with what I call the "bookends" – the realistic worst-case scenario and the realistic best-case scenario.

What if things go really well? Will there be enough product to supply the market? How much will it cost to expand capacity? How much working capital will be tied up?

What if things go really poorly? How much sunk cost will be lost? Will there be a need for employee layoffs? What are the financial implications?

Contemplate alternate outcomes – decisions rarely play out exactly as planned.

Bring your sense of humor to work

Humor is one of the most under-appreciated attributes in a work setting. When used in the right way and at the right time, it builds trust among a team and facilitates a more comfortable work environment.   It puts people at ease and gives them a sense of perspective. Humor can bring levity to an otherwise overly serious situation.

That being said, there are watchouts when it comes to workplace humor. Areas to avoid include sex, religion, stereotypes, politics, and anything that is belittling or condescending toward a specific person or group of people. Used inappropriately, humor can significantly damage strong relationships.

Laughter makes people more productive.

93 | P R A C T I C A L   A D V I C E

It's only an assignment if someone takes it

I can't tell you how many times I've been in a meeting where a topic got discussed, actions identified... and then we moved onto the next topic without documenting or assigning the actions.

As you can imagine, the success rate for ownerless actions being completed is somewhere between zero and none.

In discussions where an action is being contemplated, there's a critical point when it needs to become (1) a documented assignment or (2) consciously dropped.

If you want something done, you need to assign it to someone, even if it's to yourself.

The best time to buy a new car is when you don't need one

Negotiations are all about leverage. Whichever party has the most leverage (and knows it) will almost certainly get the better end of the deal. In a car buying setting, the ultimate leverage is your willingness to walk away without a new car.

Don't go into negotiations blind. Document what you need, what you want, and what you're willing to live with (or without). And do your best to speculate on the other party's positions and how they might play out in the negotiation.

Generously invest in negotiation preparation.

Focus on those things within your control

You can't control initiatives for which you don't have responsibility. You can't control other people's thoughts, opinions and beliefs. And you can't control the past or the future.

What you can control is your motivation, your response to situations, your effort, your attitude, how you treat people, how you spend your time, where you put your energy, your values, and your actions and reactions.

Dwelling on "uncontrollables" only leads to frustration.

There's no such thing as a strategy emergency — at least there shouldn't be

By definition, a company's strategy should have a long time horizon, be thoughtful, not rushed, and shouldn't change every year.

It's only when people treat their Strategic Plan like a "Five-Year Business Plan" that a crisis emerges,

> *"Oh my gosh, we're not going to deliver the $9.83 million revenue increase shareholders are expecting in three years. Call a meeting for 6am to develop detailed action plans...."*.

Don't mingle strategy with planning.

Don't mistake a disciplined approach for bureaucracy

I worked in large, highly regulated, multinational corporations my entire career and experienced plenty of wasteful bureaucracy. That being said, I'm an engineer at heart and, as such, have an appreciation for structure and order.

Don't let individuals or functions shun all forms of discipline in the name of fighting bureaucracy. It's really not a question of whether you need or don't need robust, repeatable, business processes, it's to what extent you need them.

Chaos prevails in the absence of structure.

A team is a collection of individuals

Even if your team is high functioning with members who work well together and are motivated by a common purpose, it's still important to treat and interact with each member as an individual.

- Know what motivates them
- Know their communication preferences
- Know their leadership style and tendencies
- Know a bit about their personal life

The highest performing teams have a blend of different personalities, backgrounds, interaction and leadership styles, etc.

Get to know your team – individually.

Ask how information or data is going to be used before providing it

The amount of readily available information and data has grown exponentially over the past few decades. With increased access comes an increased responsibility to understand the source and context of the data.

Unfortunately, this responsibility is far too often dropped in the name of speed – people looking for quick answers. The situation can be further exacerbated by the data request coming in an email or text. The person requesting the information may not even realize their ask isn't perfectly clear.

Protect your information from being abused.

You're always "on the record"

No matter how safe an environment you work in or how great a relationship you have with your boss and co-workers, people are always taking note of how you behave, how you react to stress, how you treat people, how you manage situations, etc.

It's just not possible for people to dismiss actions and be-haviors they've observed – the very ones that will be referenced when jobs are filled, promotions awarded, and assignments given.

Perceptions are reality to the observer.

You don't have to agree with a decision – but once it's made, you do need to support it

Hopefully you work with a leader who asks for input as part of their decision making process. Regardless, the leader is the one tasked with making the final decision.

While you may not agree with each and every one of these decisions, nothing positive comes from you undermining it. Your job is to help the company succeed. Do you honestly believe your dissension will reverse the decision or benefit the company in any way?

Have confidence in your leaders. Give them the benefit of the doubt that they make good decisions considering all the priorities and issues they're juggling.

Respect decisions. Give them every opportunity to succeed.

Offering someone a position in your company is a really important decision – treat it with the utmost respect

Having talented employees is critical to the success of any company, as they are a key source of competitive advantage. Attracting and hiring the right ones can be challenging and, as such, you need to put in the time and effort to do it right.

- Don't delegate the hiring process too low in the organization
- Don't rush the process
- In addition to work experience, look at talent and cultural fit
- Leverage references and check social media
- Hire for a career
- Pay attention to the questions candidates ask
- Trust your instincts

Be selective in your choice of future co-workers.

Great presentations don't happen by chance

You've got to put in the time, energy and effort to develop and deliver a compelling message.

- Know your audience
- Be yourself, be authentic
- Make eye contact, addressing the whole room
- Speak, don't read
- Be conscious of your body language
- Slow down, particularly if people with multiple native languages are in attendance
- Use visuals when needed, but don't overload them with excessive detail
- Inject humor, if appropriate
- Ask for questions

Prepare and practice.

Promotions are earned

Over the years, I've had countless discussions with individuals disappointed in their career progression. They felt they had held the right positions, put in the time and were ready to move to the next level.

In reality, their careers weren't being stifled because they lacked experience. They were just never the top candidate for a given promotion.

A promotion isn't about a checklist of roles held or activities completed. A promotion isn't awarded to a qualified candidate. It's awarded to the *most* qualified candidate.

Take actions to distinguish yourself.

Don't mistake a series of meetings for a plan

There are obviously times when teams need to gain alignment, establish plans, make decisions, etc. And a meeting
may very well be the perfect forum.

That being said, I've seen far too many times when people
respond to a specific challenge with a series of meetings
before the issue is even understood.

Assess your issue off-line and develop a tentative plan,
then schedule meetings, as needed – if needed.

Stress has gotten a bad rap – but it's not all bad

There's a big difference between chronic and short-term stress.

Chronic stress is a constant and unrelenting feeling of being pressured or overwhelmed and can seem inescapable. It's obviously unhealthy and, as such, you need to take the necessary steps to minimize or alleviate it.

Conversely, short-term stress – aka the fight or flight response – has associated benefits. It's the stress you feel when you're excited. It can boost both cognitive and physical performance and keep you alert, focused, and motivated.

Use 'good anxiety' as a catalyst for accomplishment.

Celebrate small victories

Celebrating brings out a sense of pride and happiness, which is, in turn, motivating. It keeps people tracking toward a goal.

While true success – the kind you would obviously celebrate – comes from the completion of projects, this can be months or even years into the future.

Set intermediate goals and appreciate incremental progress.

Play offense

Offense is focused on winning. It's intentional, liberating, proactive, motivating, engaging, and it creates momentum. People are energized when they get the opportunity to chart their own course.

Conversely, playing defense is playing not to lose. It's constantly reacting to outside influences and competitive pressures – e.g., cutting costs, delaying projects, halting travel and outside hiring. Over time, it takes its toll on both financial performance and employee morale.

Control your own destiny.

Don't be in too much of a hurry – unless you absolutely have to be

Emergency situations require immediate action. There's just no way around it. In these cases, you may need to accept a suboptimal solution in the name of speed.

In all other situations, be deliberate. Take your time to really think things through, ask questions, contemplate alternatives, collect data, assess the pros and cons, etc.

No awards are given for fast, poor decisions.

Just because you started a project doesn't mean you're obligated to finish it

Initiatives are approved based on information existing at the time – information which is far from perfect. As projects progress, the world changes. Market dynamics change, cost estimates and timelines are updated, new competitors enter the market, etc.

A project should always be viewed in the context of it moving forward. How much <u>more</u> money will it take? How much <u>more</u> time will it take? What other initiatives could your limited resources be allocated to?

Don't fall in love with any given project. At each update, think about whether you'd approve it in the context of today.

Sunk cost should have no bearing on whether or not you continue a project.

Execution is what separates you from the competition

You likely work for a company in an industry in which there is intense competition from one or several other companies with similar products or service offerings. And it's also likely these competitors have very similar long-term strategies.

The winners and losers are largely separated by their ability to identify and execute specific action plans and initiatives.

- Bringing new products or services to market
- Establishing the most efficient supply chains
- Attracting lucrative customers

Mission and vision statements are nice, but execution pays the bills.

It's okay to vent – to the right person and in the right way

No matter how good a company you work for or how much you love your job, you'll undoubtedly have times when you "just wanna scream".

To get through those times, you need someone to confide in, someone who won't judge you and won't feel the need to give you advice, someone who will just listen and empathize, affording you the opportunity to "spill your bucket".

Be careful to keep your venting brief as it can easily turn into complaining, which isn't productive.

Venting is therapeutic – practice it safely.

Follow the money – a simple guide to driving productivity

I assume nearly every for-profit company has some sort of goal or objective associated with driving down costs or increasing productivity.

A good starting point for identifying improvement opportunities is to assess your company's cash flow.

Meet with your Financial Controller and break down your costs in as much detail as is practical. How much money is flowing externally – e.g., utilities, raw materials? What are your fixed costs? What costs are variable with the amount of product you make or sell? How much is your labor cost?

A small percent reduction in your biggest expenses can deliver significant savings.

Don't take yourself or work too seriously

It's easy to get caught up in the daily grind, the frenzy of work activity, the stresses, endless meetings, etc. To keep your sanity, you've got to periodically step back, take a few deep breaths, and celebrate accomplishments, even if by yourself.

Put things in perspective. No matter what's going on, the sun will come up tomorrow and the business and all its issues will still be there.

The job and your company are important, but they're not everything...they don't define you.

Bosses – be aware of the amount of work you generate when you ask questions

At first blush, you might think this one is in direct contradiction to my points about asking questions and being curious – but hear me out.

In general, people want to please their bosses. They want to accommodate requests, deliver on commitments, and, yes, get answers to their questions.

An innocent text from your boss posing a question can cause a flurry of activity involving multiple people, gathering of data, analysis, etc. – well beyond what may have been intended. It's easy to text a question, not so easy for the recipient(s) to clarify the ask.

Make sure your question's answer is worth the investment it takes to get it.

You better have a really good reason to disregard the data

Data is evidence of what happened in the past – a manufacturing process yield, inventory level, or the amount of product sold last month. It's indisputable within the operating parameters existing at the time. And most importantly, it gives you insights into what is likely to happen in the future.

That being said, there are times when the past is not a good predictor of the future. If, for instance, there is a competitive entrant or significant price inflation.

If you choose to forecast something contrary to past performance, specifically note (1) what has changed and (2) why and to what extent it changes your forecast.

Don't ignore data in support of what you *want* to happen.

Be on time and well prepared for meetings

The meeting can't start until you're present, assuming you're important to the discussion (which should be the case if your valuable time has been scheduled).

Your contribution to the meeting is directly proportional to the time you've spent reviewing the pre-reads and preparing to discuss or debate your position.

Don't let your lack of preparation be the other attendees' punishment.

The best employees aren't necessarily the ones adept at getting out of a crisis

Crisis situations and the employees directly involved get a lot of attention from key leaders. The leaders have a front-row seat, witnessing individuals doing admirable work digging out of a tough spot.

With this extra attention comes familiarity and in many cases the start of long-standing relationships – ones that can lead to future career opportunities.

What about the employees who anticipate and avoid crises? Give them the attention they've earned.

Don't let delegation degrade to abdication

A hallmark of a great leader is their ability to effectively delegate, assigning and entrusting others to complete tasks on their behalf. Effective delegation comes with training, support, a due date, and routine check-ins. While the leader is not doing the task, they're still fully responsible for its completion.

Delegation becomes abdication when the task is transitioned with little to no support, communication or accountability. The lack of follow-up leaves the person receiving the assignment with unclear expectations and a feeling the task may not be important.

Routinely check on the status of delegated activity.

Emails are dangerously easy to forward

Electronic messages leave a trail and have the potential to be "out there" – forever!

Before hitting the send button, think about the content of your message as well as the tone and wording. Consider not only how it will land with the addressees, but also how it would be taken by others if it were to be forwarded.

Avoid things that could be hurtful to others. And be careful with humor and sarcasm as they are hard to convey in a note.

Never send an email or text when you're upset.

Contemplate failure to prevent it

No matter how much you want to believe a project can be executed flawlessly, it's rarely, if ever, the case. Things go wrong. There are set-backs, delays, design issues, and sometimes complete failures.

The best way to minimize the potential for failures is to proactively brainstorm things that could go wrong, and to identify and implement actions to prevent them.

When contemplating a new aircraft, you want engineers to assess the things that could cause it to fall out of the sky, well ahead of it taking flight.

Assign someone to pressure test your initiatives.

Give your employees "the right amount" of space and attention

Unfortunately, there's no universal definition for "the right amount". Every employee has a different threshold when it comes to oversight and attention from their boss.

Some employees want/need a lot of attention and constant contact. The lack of attention is seen as a lack of caring or abandonment – that they're not performing important work.

For other employees, that same level of attention would be viewed as micromanaging, or a lack of trust.

Take a tailored approach to each of your employees.

Employees will stay with your company if they are _____

- ✓ well compensated
- ✓ challenged
- ✓ promoted
- ✓ appreciated
- ✓ aligned to the company mission
- ✓ trusted
- ✓ empowered
- ✓ involved
- ✓ valued
- ✓ coached/mentored

Loyalty is your reward for treating employees well.

Don't underestimate the power of stability

Throughout my career, I've seen a great deal of time, effort, and energy put into driving change. Some of it was productive and needed to happen.   But some of it was change for the sake of change – people coming up with new and novel ways of doing things differently, but not necessarily better.

Be deliberate when contemplating change. Does it really need to be done? Does it make the situation better, or just different? Is it the best use of limited resources? Is the timing right to introduce something new?

Better execution of existing work practices may be the most impactful change.

Only use "Reply All" when absolutely necessary

I'll never understand what compels people to copy all the original email recipients with,

> *"Thanks for sending the information"*, or

> *"Thanks, I'll be there".*

Does everyone really need to know this? Remember, there's a tangible cost associated with people receiving and opening email.

Do your work colleagues a favor – don't fill their inboxes with frivolous replies.

Never ask someone to do something you'd be unwilling to do yourself

Lead by example.

Be a good steward of your company's limited resources

Your company's profitability is directly and proportion-ately impacted by the level of spending – i.e., each dollar spent is one less dollar of profit.

Adopt an owner's mentality.

- Be selective when it comes to new initiatives
- Competitively bid work
- Negotiate the best price and contract terms
- Don't spend money just because you've budgeted for it
- Eliminate unnecessary activity and expenses

Spend your company's money like it's your own.

Document decisions

It never ceases to amaze me how quickly people (including myself) forget the how's, when's and why's associated with a given decision. The obvious solution to this is to document decisions in real time. While it may seem a bit bureaucratic, it will save you time in the long run.

Things to document include:

- What is the decision?
- General background
- Why is the decision needed? Why at this time?
- Who actually had the authority and made the decision? Who supported the decision?
- Analysis completed and options considered
- Business case, financials
- Risks/benefits
- Recommendation(s) with justification
- Stakeholder and communication plan

Memorialize the time and effort you've invested in getting to a decision.

We, not me

Business is a team sport. It takes all kinds of people, diverse talents, knowledge, experiences, backgrounds, etc. for a company to be successful.

Take the time to collaborate, listening to others' ideas and incorporating their input. Be approachable and create an environment where you win as a team. Bring everyone along for the ride.

Give others credit for accomplishments.

Why do people believe overly complex business processes will actually get followed?

In an effort to cover every conceivable scenario, people feel compelled to develop complicated procedures – ones requiring an advanced degree to understand and the patience of a saint to follow.

Straightforward processes that are actually executed add far more value than complex operations that are ignored or worked around.

Invest the time and energy to "right size" your company's business processes, striking a balance between thorough-ness and executability.

Keep it simple.

Presentations are highly visible displays of your skills and abilities

Presentations are a key form of communication within most every organization. They're used to educate, to inform, to motivate... and probably most importantly, they're how initiatives are brought forward for discussion and approval.

When it's your turn to get in front of an audience, be prepared. Rightly or wrongly, a lot of conclusions about your broader capabilities (including upward potential) are extrapolated from your ability to deliver a crisp, concise, logical message in front of a group.

- Communication skills... obviously
- Ability to analyze situations
- Judgment
- Use of data
- Organizational skills
- Ability to "think on your feet"
- Leadership and influence

Be prepared – don't let a poor public showing diminish your work or tarnish your reputation.

Nurture *constructive* dissent – it's a product of knowledge and passion

It takes a lot of guts, conviction, and energy to go against the prevailing winds, to be a holdout, poking holes in a proposal – especially if said proposal is coming directly from "the boss".

But the lack disagreement and open discussion deprives the group of valuable information. And sometimes the minority position is actually right!

Bosses, encourage a "speak-up" culture. Establish rules of engagement to draw out differing perspectives while preserving relationships. And publicly praise those willing to raise an uncomfortable topic or position.

Choose your battles, then go to battle – constructively.

Make sure you have passions outside of work

Work can certainly be your passion, maybe even your number one passion. Just don't let it be your only one.

Find something else, something that gives you satisfaction and an outlet from the pressures of work. Go camping. Take up golf. Travel abroad. Spend time with friends and family. Plant a garden. Support the arts. Invent something. Build something. Pick up a musical instrument.

Extracurricular activities obviously become more important as you near retirement, when you'll be able to devote more time to those things that were previously pastimes.

Learn to play.

Keep this book handy…

…. as a constant reminder of the simple things you can do to be more successful.

Sage advice has no expiration date.

Quick Guide

21 Just because your spreadsheet can handle numbers with lots of decimal points doesn't mean you should show them

22 Every company should have a Commonsense Committee

23 Sleep is a prerequisite to productive waking hours

24 Don't let arrogance be your downfall

25 Your best attribute in excess is likely your greatest weakness

26 The greatest compliment a technical expert can receive shouldn't be a management position

27 You can't say you're on *[plan, schedule, budget]* if you don't have one

28 Strive for consistency

29 You're unlikely to get to your career destination without a map

30 Schedule uninterrupted time – it doesn't happen naturally

31 There's nothing wrong with a judgment call – just don't make people invent data to support it

32 Do you demonstrate a work/life balance?

33 Save meeting time by recognizing when you're in violent agreement

34 If someone has to tell you they're being *[transparent, humble, vulnerable, etc.]*, it's because they're typically not

35 The message is more important than the slides, but you do want to look professional

36 Encourage and reward replication

37 Be a bit skeptical of percentages

38 Ambiguity in the workplace is inevitable – you better get comfortable navigating it

Index

V

W